From that moment on, the city on the Tagus gradually grew up and took on a new appearance, going beyond the confines of its walled precinct. Lisbon became the capital of the kingdom of Portugal in the 13th century, entering into a period of splendour that reached its zenith when, at the beginning of the period of Atlantic expansion and the discovery of Brazil and the trade route to the Indies, it became the most important port in the world.

In 1755, Lisbon lived through tragic moments when it was devastated by a colossal earthquake. The mediaeval part of Lisbon was completely destroyed, excepting the picturesque Alfama district. The city was rebuilt under the dynamic and intelligent direction of the Marquis de Pombal, and a new Lisbon was created according to a geometrical urban design. The lines established by Pombal largely determined the subsequent growth of this lovely city and Lisbon, without losing its charming, characteristic aspect, became the great modern city it is today.

Glazed tiles commemorating the conquest of Lisbon.

Pavilion of the Oceans.

THE CITY

Main focus of Portugal's social, economic and cultural development, Lisbon is a city of beautiful contrasts, from its seven hills overlooking the immense estuary of the River Tagus. Spectacularly tinged by the golden tones emanating from the generous sun's sparkling dance on the water, the Portuguese capital gazes towards the Atlantic Ocean, whose routes it dominated in by-gone times and along which it is still an important port of call. It was from Lisbon's port that countless expeditions to the Indies and voyages discovery set out, and it is for this reason that the 1998 Universal Exhibition, held in the Portuguese capital, took as its central theme that of the oceans.

A city in constant growth, today's Lisbon combines the seductive beauty of its historic districts with the modernity and attractiveness of peripheral zones of more recent construction. Walking around the picturesque streets of the mediaeval Alfama quarter or contemplating the historic old palaces of São Cristóvão is no less stimulating than visiting the urban development brought into being as a result of Lisbon's nomination as the host city to the last Universal Exhibition of the 20th century. The zone chosen as the site of this work was the eastern part of the city, then occupied by military warehouses, a refinery, a slaughterhouse and a waste dump. Along a five-kilometre stretch of the river bank were built, as well as the Expo'98 pavilions, a park, a residential zone with complete services, a station, given the name of Oriente, where the main means of transport in the region converge, and the splendid new Vasco

ALL LISBON
AND ITS SURROUNDINGS

Editorial Escudo de Oro, S.A.

Historic engraving of Lisbon in the City Museum.

LISBON, MUCH-PRAISED CITY...

Long before Lisbon attained the status of Roman municipality in the I century AD, both Phoenicians and Carthaginians had made their way there. Situated in a truly privileged location atop hills and on the banks of the Tagus, whose magnificent estuary it overlooks, the city was inhabited at least 2,500 years before the birth of Christ, as is shown by Bronze Age remains found in the beautiful area where Lisbon now stands.

The great Portuguese poet of the «saudade», Teixeira de Pascoaes, described in enamoured verse the unique situation of the evocative capital of Portugal:

Surge Lisboa, branca, ao pé do Tejo azul;
A Lisboa das naus,
Constraida em marfim, sobre colinas de oiro.
Vede o imenso estuário... (é sonho ou realidade?)
Sob um Azul divino a desfolhar-se em asas!

Lisbon, the Atlantic city beloved of poets, fully deserves the honour of the immortal Camões' invention of the charming legend that it was founded by none other than Ulysses. After a period of Roman domination –known to the Roman world firstly as *Olisipo* and, later, *Felicitas Julia*– Lisbon was occupied by Aluns, Suevians, Visigoths and Arabs, being conquered by the Christian hosts of Afonso Henriques, the first Portuguese king, in the year 1147.

da Gama bridge, as much a prodigy of civil engineering as the famed 25 de Abril bridge was in its day. Other legacies of this important event are the pavilions of the Oceans, Virtual Reality and Utopia. The first, designed by the North American architect Peter Chermayeff, remains operational and is now one of the largest oceanariums in the world. In it are represented four of the world's coastal zone types, corresponding to the marine environment of the Indian, Pacific, Antarctic and Atlantic oceans. The Ocean Pavilion is estimated to receive almost one million visitors per year.

For its part, the Virtual Reality Pavilion is a cyberpark welcoming visitors into a fascinating world of illusion recreated by the new technologies, and also remained open to the public after the closure of Expo'98. Also worthy of mention apart is the Utopia Pavilion, converted into a multi-purpose facility at the service of the city of Lisbon and considered the most notable of the pavilions from an architectural point of view. Semicircular in form, its interior lined by sheets of Swedish pinewood, the building is the work of Portuguese architect Regino Cruz. Heated, cooled, air-conditioned and lighted using natural energy sources, the pavilion has a modern amphitheatre seating 12,000 extendible 16,000.

The most outstanding element of Oriente Station, designed by the Spanish architect Santiago Cala-

Oriente Station.

The Amoreiras shopping centre.

trava, is its steel and glass roof, supported by the branches of metallic trees. The inspiration behind this concept are the many trees found in the city of Lisbon. The site is a combined railway, bus and coach and metro station, as well as being linked to the airport.

Another example of the renovating spirit with which the Portuguese capital is currently imbued is the Amoreiras shopping centre, situated in Avenida Duarte Pacheco, and whose silhouette is highly visible from all parts of the city. The centre is housed in an enormous post-modern building containing a complete range of commercial and leisure services: a ten-screen cinema, around 60 restaurants, a hotel and more than 300 shops.

But Lisbon also means tradition, history, an age-old flavour and air. The oldest part of the city clusters around the Castle of São Jorge (St. George's Castle), the site of the original city. When Christian forces expelled the Moors in 1147, a first extension of original nucleus began with the construction of the picturesque mediaeval Alfama quarter. These hilltop streets command views over the two Lisbons, the modern and historic cities, intertwined in a harmonious embrace. Little by little, the city centre gradually shifted towards the River Tagus. Nevertheless, the devastating earthquake of 1755 brought this growth to a brusque halt and led to the adoption of a more rational, geometric urban layout according to the directives of the Marquis of Pombal, King José I's prime minister. Besides the Alfama district, with its labyrinth of narrow streets, the Bairro Alto, a quarter rich in history and folklore, and the São Cristóvão district, its streets lined by old palaces, also survived the cataclysm.

The city seen from St. George's Castle.

Figueira Square, seen from St George's Castle.

Praça do Comercio.

Another particularly interesting part of Lisbon is the area known as «Baixa», which extends between the bustling Rossio and Comerçio squares. The first of these was witness to some of the most important events in the city's history, whilst Praça do Comerçio, presided over by the equestrian statue of King José I, is outstanding due to the fine equilibrium of its proportions and enormous size.

Though partially destroyed by fire in 1988, the Chiado quarter continues to be one of the city's most attractive areas. Many of its winding streets and tiny squares contain elegant shops and fine coffee-shops which were once important meeting-places, as well as a source of inspiration for some of the most prestigious figures in Portuguese letters.

Beside Rossio Station, whose construction goes back to the 19th century, in the square of the same name, stands the Monument to the Restorers, a 30-metre high obelisk erected to commemorate the revolution of 1640, which culminated with the independence of Portugal, which had been under Spanish rule for the preceding 50 years. This square also marks the starting-point of Avenida da Liberdade, the city's main artery, flanked by rows of trees and fountains. At its highest point stands the bronze statue of the Marquis of Pombal, artifice of the reconstruction of Lisbon after the earthquake of 1755.

Also of outstanding interest are the parks and gardens scattered amongst the urban areas of the city. Particular mention should be made here of the Botanical Gardens, founded in 1875, with its gigantic greenhouses; the Monsanto Forestry Park, populated by cedar, cypress, eucalyptus and oak and commanding fine views of the Tagus; the tropical

Arco da Rua Augusta, leading into Praça do Comerçio.

The City Chamber, built in 1864 according to the neo-classical model, houses the Historic Archive. The building stands in the splendid Praça do Municipio, in whose centre stands the pillory, an old instrument of punishment now converted into a symbol of civil liberties.

gardens known as the *Estufa Fría*, where species characteristic of other latitudes are cultivated; and many more, including the Jardim da Estrela and the Zoological Gardens.

But Lisbon is also its people: happy, sentimental, polite and full of good cheer, romantic and hospitable. The charm of its inhabitants adds even more, if this is possible, to the enormous power of attraction of a city which is looking boldly and decidedly towards the future whilst conserving its past with love and pride.

Typical Lisbon tram.

CONVENT OF O CARMO

Considered the veritable jewel in the crown of Lisbon Gothic, the Convent of O Carmo was built at the orders of Condestable Nuno Álvares Pereira between the late-14th and early-15th centuries. This soldier, who fought in the armies of King Joan I, had promised to built a magnificent sanctuary if granted victory at the Battle of Aljubarrota at which, as it turned out, the Portuguese armies indeed emerged victories against the Spanish forces. Besides being of undeniable architectural beauty, the Convent also houses many treasures of the highest value. With the passing of time, it became the most popular church in Lisbon and a place of pilgrimage for the faithful throughout Portugal, who came here to pray at the tomb of Nuno Álvares Pereira, who died just a few years after the completion of the Convent. The earthquake which devastated the city in 1755 left it seriously damaged, and only a few walls and some of the ogee arches of the nave and two aisles into which the interior was divided survived. Despite its ruinous state, however, the building still conserves an impressive aspect, and its shape can be seen from many points in the city.

Towards the end of the last century, it was decided to install a small but important archaeological museum on the convent site, and this museum now contains fascinating collections of tombs, sculptures, engravings and escutcheons.

The Gothic ruins of the Church of the Convent of O Carmo.

Santa Justa lift.

THE SANTA JUSTA LIFT

Lisbon's Bairro Alto district resembles Alfama in its steep streets and in having escaped serious damage at the hands of the 1755 earthquake. Here, too, visitors to the city are often serenaded by the lilting tones of a *fado.* Strolling around the Bairro Alto gives us the opportunity of admiring the typical wrought-iron railings of the balconies and to delight in the characteristic layout of its streets. It is precisely the unique structure of the Bairro Alto district which led to it being provided with one of the most popular means of transport in Lisbon: the funicular railway and the Santa Justa lift. There are at present three funicular railway lines helping travellers over the steep rises and falls of the zone, the oldest, known as the Elevador do Lavra, was built in 1884.

For its part, the Santa Justa lift links Rua do Ouro and O Carmo hill, separated one from another by a distance of 32 metres. The great iron tower housing the lift reaches a total height of 45 metres. Built in neo-Gothic style, it entered into service in 1902 and is the work of the Portuguese engineer Raúl Mesnier du Ponsard, a disciple of G. Eiffel. The lift is crowned by a viaduct giving access to Largo do Carmo.

ROSSIO SQUARE (PRAÇA DO ROSSIO)

A superb square... large, beautiful and well laid-out, according to Tirso de Molina's just description of it, in which all the history and all the dynamic present of Lisbon are concentrated, with the statue of Peter IV, the first constitutional king of Portugal, in the centre, dominating from his pedestal the front of the National Theatre and the Church of São Domingos, the largest in Lisbon, whose nave is supported by fine pink marble columns.

Rossio Square, with its fountains, florists', kiosks –where you can buy any European newspaper– its cafes and curious railway station

The popular Rossio railway station.

close by, is a truly stimulating human scene. In Rossio all is movement, everything seems to be imbued with the uncontrollable desire to live freely, to breathe deeply of the most intense vital aromas. Swarms of people are constantly going from one part to another. Everyone looks and is looked at –but here the looks are not offensive, they merely seem to greet us in a friendly fashion– throughout the length and breadth of this delightful square, the only part of Lisbon destroyed by the 1755 earthquake that was not rebuilt, and therefore still largely preserving its pre-Pombalian appearance.

It was right here, in Rossio Square, where the aristocrats who lived in St. George's Castle, the merchants established in the environs of the port and the common people first began to live together democratically. Before urbanisation, O Rossio was a plot of land where cattle markets and horse races were held; it was also used for slaughtering pigs. This open space in the city became so popular with the people of Lisbon that in the 13th century, when King Dinis wanted to build slaughterhouses and shops there, the city council took the monarch to court to defend the right of the people to have Rossio continue to exist as an open space. The history of the square to a large extent mirrors that of the city as regards both everyday customs and important events. In former times, the high class citizens of Lisbon watered their horses in O Rossio, looked longingly at the girls walking by, and commented on the latest court stories and gossip.

One turbulent night, during a period of popular uprisings, the Mestre de Aviz was acclaimed as king in Rossio Square. Another historic event that took place in O Rossio was on Easter Day 1506, when a terrible slaughter lasting three days took place, resulting in the death of two thousand Jews and heretics.

The Palace of the Inquisition formerly stood in the square on the same spot as the present site of the theatre whose first director was the famous Portuguese playwright Gil Vicente.

In the pink-toned palace beside the Municipal

Rossio Square.

Praça da Figueira, with St George's Castle in the background.

Theatre a historic conspiracy of Portuguese nobles took place on 1 December 1640, sparking off events which led to the country's independence from Spain. O Rossio was always, throughout the ages, the centre for all types of political conspiracies, sometimes against the monarchy, others against the Republic, and later against Salazar.

The real name of Rossio Square is Pedro IV Square, named after the king whose statue stands in its centre with a gesture offering the people of Lisbon a liberal constitution conceived and drawn in Brazil. But the will of the people has irrevocably named the square Praça do Rossio, and it is known by this name to one and all.

FIGUEIRA SQUARE

This square adjoins Praça do Rossio and is surrounded by streets full of bars and popular restaurants serving the delicious wines of the country, as well as high quality old brandy.

The atmosphere of Figueira Square (Praça da Figueira) is not as bustling and dynamic as O Rossio. It is calmer here, but the popular and the historical are also inextricably intermingled.

In the centre of Figueira Square stands the equestrian statue of Don João I, and from the opposite corner to the castle, the unmistakable pile of St. George's castle can be seen on the horizon.

Interior of the Museum of Saint Anthony, and a statue of Saint Anthony, patron saint of Lisbon.

CHURCH OF SAINT ANTHONY

This church, which lies near the cathedral, on the site where the Senate once stood, belongs to the City Chamber. The church was built in honour of the city's most popular and venerated saint, born in September 1191, the son of Teresa and Martinho. It still preserves the crypt where, according to tradition, the Portuguese saint baptised as Fernando de Bulhões was born, later to die in Padua, by which time he had been converted into Saint Anthony. Legend has it that when the Saint died, all the bells of Lisbon spontaneously began to toll for the dead man. When the original church was destroyed by an earthquake, its reconstruction was paid for by donations and alms given by the people of Lisbon to children collecting from door to door. The work of rebuilding the Church of Santo António was directed by Mateus Vicente, the architect who also built the Basilica da Estrela in Lisbon, and the Queluz Palace.

*Façade of
the Church
of Saint
Anthony.*

Chapel of Charola and the tomb of Lopo Fernandes Pacheco.

Cathedral cloister.

Front of Lisbon Cathedral. ▷

THE CATHEDRAL

This is one of Lisbon's most ancient monuments. The popular *Sé* (See), built during the reigns of Afonso Henriques and Sancho I, was rebuilt in different periods after having been partially destroyed by various earth tremors. Nevertheless, its original Romanesque construction still preserves much of its purity of style. Apparently, the Englishman, Gilbert Hastings, who was to be the first bishop of Lisbon, was one of the most active promoters of the construction of Lisbon Cathedral.

The cloister and the Chapel of Joanes are of Gothic inspiration. Outstanding for their beauty are the Romanesque windows in the façade and the vaults in the same style over the nave, also the Sacristy, the funeral stones –especially that of the tomb of Lopo Fernandes Pacheco– the richly-adorned Romanesque grille closing off one of the chapels in the beautifully-adorned Gothic cloister, the transept and the ambulatory, with its tombs and apse chapels.

The structure of the cathedral has rather the look of a mediaeval fortress. Partially destroyed by the 1755 earthquake, reconstruction was not completed until 1940. Its lovely outline stands out elegantly not far from the curious Casa dos Bicos and the Church of Saint Anthony, close to the Tagus.

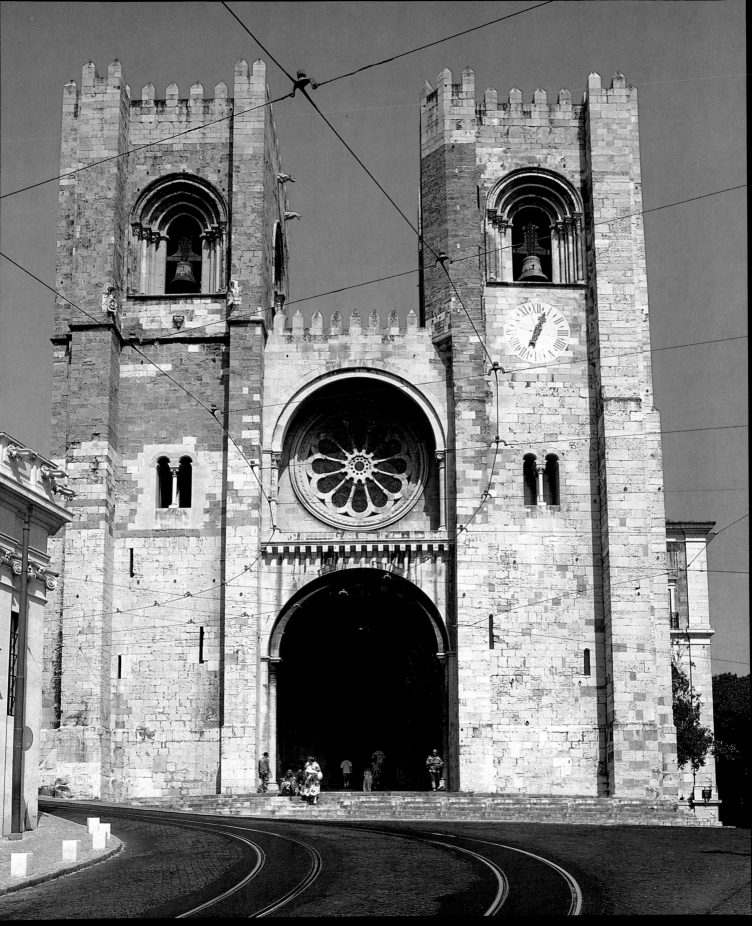

Façade of the popular Casa dos Bicos.

THE CASA DOS BICOS

Also known as the Casa dos Diamantes (House of Diamonds), this unusual palace was built by Don Bras, son of the famous Don Afonso de Alburquerque, Governor of Portuguese India in the 16th century. The house is in Renaissance style, diamond shapes forming the principal decorative motif on the front. The polycentric arches of the doors are in Manueline style.

The Casa dos Bicos was partially destroyed by the 1755 earthquake, after which only two of its four original floors were rebuilt. The palace was eventually restored, the two remaining storeys rebuilt, in 1983. The façade is reminiscent of those of the Casa de los Picos in Segovia, and the Pallazo dei Diamanti in Ferrara.

SAINT GEORGE'S CASTLE

Standing on the highest hill overlooking the Tagus estuary, this privileged spot commands views over the whole of the Lisbon area, whilst the castle itself, with its romantic architectural impact, can be seen from any part of the city.

St. George's Castle was built before the foundation of the Portuguese nation and is Lisbon's most ancient monument.

A royal residence from the time of Afonso Henriques to the reign of Manuel I, it still preserves the walls surrounding the fortress and the gateway where Martim Moniz lost his life bravely fighting against the Moors who defended the proud castle, near to which is the Church of Santa Cruz, built on the site of a former mosque.

Partial view of St. George's Castle.

Beside the castle is the statue of St. George, at whose service there was always a horse chosen from amongst the finest in the kingdom, in memory of the fact that King Sancho bequeathed the Saint his own mount when he died.

The terraces and towers of this imposing mediaeval fortress –beautifully reconstructed in 1947 to commemorate eighth centenary of the Christian conquest of Lisbon– make a fine vantage point from which to enjoy magnificent panoramic views, with the Tagus and the whole city stretching out beneath: a real feast for the eyes.

Panoramic view of St. George's Castle.

Partial view of the Port of Lisbon and its maritime station.

THE PORT

Lisbon has one of the most important ports in the world, a vital centre for sea communications between Europe, Africa, and America. The quays, docks and goods warehouses in the port of Lisbon occupy a total area of no less than two million square metres. This enormous port forms an estuary of colossal dimensions.

The Santa Catarina viewpoint commands a vast, impressive panoramic view comprising the Tagus, the docks and the port of Lisbon. The view from high up on the 25th of April Bridge is equally magnificent.

To go down to the port of Lisbon from the steep little streets in of A Bica district is to enjoy a unique spectacle. Irregular stone staircases appear everywhere and our view of the Tagus estuary changes continually like the images of some fabulous kaleidoscope. Down below, the river scene is densely populated with cranes, masts and sails, swaying gently in time to the movement of the water, stirred by the breeze softly blowing around the port.

In the streets surrounding the port are many bars, beer houses, sea food bars, restaurants and night clubs. The atmosphere is at once cosmopolitan and popular, flavoured with typical elements around the Duque da Terceira Square –presided over by the statue of the Liberator of Lisbon, which seems to control the busy coming and going of the picturesque trams– and the bustling streets of Bernardino Costa, Alecrim, Remolares and Nova do Carvalho.

The port of Lisbon is one the great attractions of the city which one 19th-century Portuguese poet, João de Lemos, called: *Princesa dos vastos mares.*

LISBON'S BRIDGES

At the end of its long course, having crossed half of Spain, the River Tagus finally reaches Lisbon, forming an estuary known as the «Sea of Straw». The name is an allusion to the golden reflections of the sun shining on the deep waters of the river here where, just a few metres downstream awaits the immense Ocean, from where representatives from many peoples, cultures and civilisations entered the city to form part of the commercial traffic typical of cities with river ports. All this makes the Portuguese capital's identification with the Tagus absolute. *Cidade-río* (river-city), Mário Dias Ramos called Lisbon in the title of a poem in his book Morfogenia. The Tagus embraces Lisbon in its arm of water, 15 kilometres in length, and the presence of the great river is perceptible from all parts of the city. Until 1966, it was only possible to cross between the two river banks on which the city lies by ferry, but that year saw the opening of the 20 de Abril bridge, a modern construction of iron and asphalt finally an-

Partial view of Lisbon with the Tagus in the background.

swering the age-old prayers of the people of Lisbon. In fact, the first plans for a bridge over the Tagus here date to 1876, though work did not finally begin until 1962, carried out by the same company as that which built the famous Golden Gate and Bay bridges in San Francisco, USA. The similarities between them is, therefore, not the fruit of coincidence. Two-and-a-half kilometres in length, the 20 de Abril bridge was in its time the longest in Europe. Rising 60 metres over the river, it also offers some of the most lovely views of Lisbon that one could wish for.

The bridge was originally baptised in honour of Salazar, the dictator who ruled Portugal in those times. Nevertheless, the Revolution of the Carnations, which began on 25 April 1974, as well as abruptly ending the mandate of the then president of the nation, also led to the bridge's name being changed.

The construction of the 25 de Abril bridge, spanning a narrower section of the river estuary, gave a considerable boost to the city. With its entry into service, the south bank finally ended years of isola-

25 de Abril bridge.

Vasco da Gama bridge.

tion and was able to start playing a more active role in the life of the city. Moreover, the bridge provided the inhabitants of the capital with a much quicker route to the beaches of Caparica, one of the favourite resorts of the people of Lisbon.

But, if the construction of the 25 de Abril bridge was a challenge to the civil engineering technologies of the time, none the less so was that of the Vasco da Gama bridge, opened in 1998 as part of the works carried out in the city on the occasion of the Universal Exhibition. This bridge is a full 16 kilometres in length, 13 of them over the water. Situated in the northern zone of Lisbon, close to the airport, the new bridge greatly improved communications in the city itself and between Lisbon and the rest of the country.

Though both of these bridges efficiently perform their mission of facilitating the quick and easy crossing of the river, it continues to be an authentic pleasure to sail across the Tagus on a pleasure boat. In the middle of the estuary, from where it is difficult to be sure where the river mouth actually lies, our enthralled gaze is captivated by the immense mirror of the water.

CHURCH OF SÃO VICENTE DE FORA

This is one of the churches in which the balanced style of Portuguese Renaissance architecture is most faithfully reflected. The Church of São Vicente, whose construction was directed by the Italian architect Terzi, has a façade with three porticoes and two towers of elegant, measured design and evident Roman influence.

The church was built in honour of a saint who formerly enjoyed great popularity in Lisbon. A delightful legend states that in 1173, a boat without oars or oarsmen ran aground in one of ramifications of the Tagus, guided by a pair of crows, and in it was the body of Saint Vincent, who had been tortured by the Moors in the lands of Algarve. After the saint's remains had been taken to a safe place, the two crows flew towards Lisbon Cathedral and made their nest in one of its towers.

Front of the Church of São Vicente de Fora and statue of that popular Lisbon saint.

National Pantheon.

CHURCH OF SANTA ENGRACIA

Also known as the National Pantheon, the Church of Santa Engrácia is one of the finest exponents of Portuguese baroque. It began to be built in the 17th century, and its interior was reorganised in the 1660s to suit it as a pantheon for illustrious Portuguese personages. In fact, remodelling work has gone on almost constantly throughout the 300 years or so of the church's existence. This is reflected in the popular saying «building Santa Engrácia», used by the people of Lisbon to refer to a task or undertaking which seems endless.

This great marble building is crowned by a dome at whose base, situated at a height of some 80 metres, is reached by a lift. The enormous terrace affords fine panoramic views of the city and the Tagus.

The porch of the main entrance is framed by four powerful columns, whilst the interior distribution obeys the classical design of ground plan in the form of a Greek cross and nave and three aisles culminating in a semicircle.

LADRA FAIR

The popular Ladra Fair –the oldest in the city– has taken place in Lisbon each Tuesday and Saturday since 1882. On fair day, the Campo de Santa Clara and the environs of São Vicente de Fora and Santa Engrácia become a veritable bee-hive of activity, thronged by shoppers keen to purchase articles displayed on the stalls of this flea market.

The origins of this traditional fair are unknown, though a clue may be provided in the fact that in Portuguese *ladra* means thief. What is known is that the fair took place as long ago as the early days after the Christian Reconquest of Lisbon.

Various views of the Ladra fair.

The Alfama district.

ALFAMA

Chaos and beauty go hand-in-hand in this historic quarter of the city, for many the most picturesque, fascinating and characteristic of Lisbon. A mesh of narrow, winding streets, tiny courtyards, staircases and sidestreets often leading nowhere form a veritable labyrinth whose magic enchants all those who enter. The first houses were built here during the times of the Visigoths, though the urban layout which has survived the passing of the centuries dates to the period of Moorish rule, and the very name of the areas, Alfama, derives from the Arabic «al-hamma», meaning hot water springs. After the reconquest by Christian forces, in the 13th and 14th centuries the quarter housed the humble families of fishermen and sailors. In the 16th, members of the Portuguese nobility began to establish their residences in Alfama, attracted by the enchantment emanated by every nook and cranny in the quarter. Alfama was one of the few parts of the city to be spared from the massive destruction caused by the 1755 earthquake.

To venture into the streets of Alfama is to journey back in time. Many of its dwellings, some of them built as far back as the 16th century, lean so much as to appear to defy the laws of gravity. The roofs of some buildings even touch those of the houses opposite. At day's end, *fados* fill the ears of those who wander the streets of Alfama with melancholy melodies. During the feasts for the popular patron saints in June, the balconies of the district are tinged with the colour of basil, and the streets are adorned with paper balloons.

Praça Martin Moniz.

Saint Jerome, *by Dürer, in the Museum of Ancient Art.* ▷

MUSEUM OF ANCIENT ART

It is installed in a magnificent palace not far from the Tagus and close to the former Royal Palace. Among the main pictorial works in this «Museum with the Green Windows», as it is also known, are: *The Temptation of St. Anthony,* one of Hieronymus Bosch's most famous paintings; *The Fountain of Life,* by Holbein; *St. Jerome,* by Dürer, paintings by Velazquez (who was of Portuguese descent) and Ribera, and the fine collection of early Portuguese painting, particularly the excellent panels by Nuno Gonçalves which make up the famous *Polyptic of St. Vincent,* an interesting allegory in which soldiers, merchants, friars, townsfolk, knights and princes surround the patron saint of Lisbon in a varied multitude which includes the Infante Don Henrique the Navigator.

Other works of interest are: the richly decorated monstrance worked in gold brought from Quiloa by Gil Vicente, altarpieces from different convents and monasteries in the country, silver plates –the finest in Europe– and other jewels; also, collections of pottery and tapestries. Also worthy of mention are the many sculptures which further enrich the artistic content of the museum.

The Museum of Ancient Art is situated in the Rua das Janelas Verdes, which means the Street of the Green Windows, a name that reminds one of the poem by José Newton entitled «*De uma janela de Lisboa, em manhã de Maio»,* which begins with the lovely verse: *Do curvo céu, no fundo azul, há nuvens...*

The Temptations of Saint Anthony, *by Hieronymus Bosch, in the Museum of Ancient Art.*

Polyptych of the Child, *by Nuno Gonçalves.*

THE PALACE OF AS NECESSIDADES

This former royal palace was built between 1745 and 1750 at the command of King Don João V. The architect Caetano Tomás de Sousa directed work on the building. This was the official residence of the rulers of Portugal until, with the departure of Don Manuel II in 1910, the monarchy was abolished. The Palace of As Necessidades is now the seat of the Foreign Ministry. Of particular note are the magnificent gardens surrounding the palace, which contain a varied collection of exotic plants. The works of art formerly decorating the interior of the Palace of As Necessidades are now distributed amongst different museums throughout Portugal and in the palaces of Ajuda, Queluz, and Sintra.

The building stands in the street of the same name, in the centre of which is a fountain dating from 1747, in the shape of an obelisk.

Not far from the Palace of As Necessidades is the Church of São Francisco de Paula, where we find the tomb of Dona Mariana Vitória, the wife of José I.

Façade of the Palace of As Necessidades.

Two views of the Monastery of Os Jerónimos.

OS JERÓNIMOS

The Monastery and Church of the Hieronymites (Os Jerónimos) –true marvels of Portuguese Renaissance art– were built in the early 16th century on the site formerly occupied by the altar erected in honour of Our Lady of the Navigators, before which Vasco da Gama passed in prayer the whole night before he set out on his historic voyage to the Indies.

The wealth brought by Vasco da Gama from the lands he discovered were for the most part devoted to building the splendid Hieronymite site. Miraculously spared from the devastation of the 1755 earthquake, it is the most valuable and representative monument of the Manueline period. The

Entrance to the Church of Os Jerónimos. ▷

Partial view of the elegant cloister of Os Jerónimos.

Nave in the Church of Os Jerónimos. ▷

Gothic and Renaissance styles are harmoniously combined in Os Jerónimos. The soaring beauty of the great southern door of the church facing the Tagus forcibly commands our attention, as does the portal on the side of the bridge with its magnificent architectural filigree work, the vault with its elegant pillars, and the decorative cloister. Altogether, such exuberant artistic wealth goes to create a successfully-achieved and markedly personal work of art.

Amongst the tombs in the nave, the most outstanding are those of Fernando Pessoa, Vasco da Gama and Camões, the latter empty since 1755, the year when the terrible earthquake caused the ashes of the poetic genius of *Os Lusiadas* to be scattered to the four winds.

It was until relatively recently that a procession of cod fishermen used to depart from the south entrance of the Church of the Hieronymites to invoke the protection of the Virgin before setting forth on their ocean voyage.

The interior of the church is lit by sunlight just as if its walls were miraculously transparent. The light comes from the high dome which pours daylight into the interior of the Church of Os Jerónimos, whose columns have a romantic pallor comparable to that of stalagmites.

Vasco da Gama and his sailors, when preparing to set off on their adventure to the far-off lands that were to become part of the Portuguese empire, one of the largest in the world, after paying their respects to the king, went to bow before the statue of Our Lady of the Hieronymites to ask for good fortune to accompany them on their travels.

View of the Bethlehem Tower.

Monument to the discoveries and to the Infante don Henrique, in Belém. ▷

THE BETHLEHEM TOWER (TORRE DE BELEM)

Built between the years 1515 and 1521, the Bethlehem Tower, a fortress overlooking the Tagus estuary, is one of the most characteristic monuments of the splendid Manueline period. The decoration of its elegant tower features a variety of elements representing the sea-faring spirit of the Portuguese people, and the building itself is an excellent representation of the symbolic essence of the reign of Don Manuel the Fortunate.

It is the balanced proportions of the architectural line that is most impressive in this building, designed by the great artist Francisco de Arruda. The severe military design of the exterior is in perfect harmony with the subtle grace of the Gothic interior precinct.

The Bethlehem Tower, whose battlements formerly arose right over the Tagus, is one of the most endearingly characteristic views in Lisbon and a place much frequented by tourists.

The old fortress has preserved all the grace of its Moorish domes, its lovely balconies and, most of all, that poetic aura of the past emanating from this unique white-walled monumental building.

Near the Bethlehem Tower, the Monument to the Discoveries, standing 52 metres in height, forms a tribute made by the people of Lisbon to all the brave Portuguese who took part in the great ocean crossings in the 15th and 16th centuries. Built in 1960, its design resembles the prow of a ship about to sail.

Naval museum.

NAVAL MUSEUM

It stands in the Praça do Imperia. The museum houses some interesting collections of caravels, boats, and all types of Portuguese sailing vessels, along with models of ships, artillery pieces, weapons, uniforms, and naval instruments of all kinds and all periods of history.

The collection of royal galleons is worthy of special mention, as is the sextant invented by Gago Coutinho and the first hydroplane in which the latter and his companion Sacadura Cabral crossed the Atlantic by air for the first time.

The Naval Museum is situated in one of the most attractive spots in the city, in a pleasant, well-laid-out area with an ample modern structure, to which the presence of the lovely Church of the Jerónimos and the proximity of the Torre de Belém lend historical and artistic prestige. The enterprising Portuguese spirit is ever present in the rooms of this museum, and when contemplating these old ships, cannon and other navy weapons, it is not difficult to evoke the prodigious courage that inspired the Portuguese, the inhabitants of a small but admirable country, to discover and conquer vast lands situated thousands of miles from the coasts of Portugal, and to create an empire of an impressive size and hold on to it tenaciously for centuries, right up to the 20th century, in fact. A visit to Lisbon's Naval Museum provides and excellent vision and understanding of the greatness of an illustrious people who made a glorious mark on history through their courage and industry.

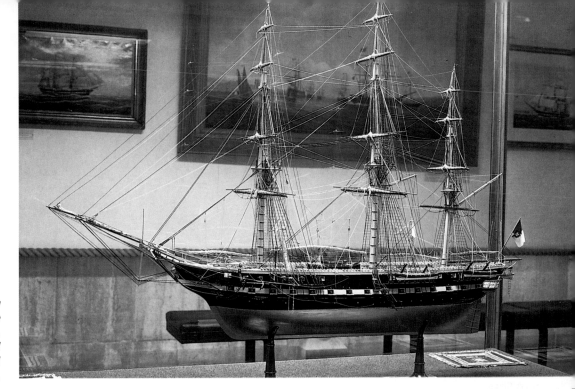

The Naval Museum contains a large collection of boats, models and nautical equipment from all periods of history.

One of the rooms in the National Museum of Archaeology and Ethnology.

NATIONAL MUSEUM OF ARCHAEOLOGY AND ETHNOLOGY

The present National Museum of Archaeology and Ethnology (The Dr. Leite de Vasconcelos Museum) was founded by Dr. José Leite de Vasconcelos Pereira de Melo in 1893 under the name of «Portuguese Ethnographic Museum». In keeping with the scientific spirit of the times, this museum was designed to house exhibits illustrating the everyday life of the people of Portugal as well as helping them to discover their origins through objects from all periods of the history of the country in a permanent exhibition. With this aim in mind, the original departments of the museum (prehistoric and historical archaeology, plus modern ethnography) were extended by the addition of ancient and modern anthropology and a comparative anthropology department.

In 1897, the museum was renamed the «Portuguese Ethnological Museum». In 1903, it was installed in its present building (the Hieronymite Monastery), and was opened to the public on 22 April 1905. Since that day, the Portuguese Ethnological Museum has become one of the most important and prestigious institutions in archaeological and ethnological research both at home and abroad. In 1928, José Leite de Vasconcelos was succeeded by Professor Manuel Helena, and the Museum's name was changed to «The Dr. Leite de Vasconcelos Ethnological Museum», in honour of its founder. Both the new director and his successor, Professor D. Fernando de Almeida, provided the driving force behind archaeological studies in the Museum by organising archaeological digs all over the country. The resulting finds were brought in to the museum, thus tipping the balance strongly in favour of the archaeological section to the detriment of other collections, more specifically that of ethnography.

Under the directorship of Professor D. Fernando de Almeida, the Museum received the name it still holds today: the «National Museum of Archaeology and Ethnography – The Dr. Leite de Vasconcelos Ethnological Museum». Various factors caused the Museum to be closed in 1979, but it was soon reopened to the public in 1980. From that year on, under the directorship of Dr. Francisco J. S. Alves, the museum underwent thorough reorganisation as regards the collections and specific departments, as well as the conservation and preservation departments. New departments were also created, such as the Paleo-ecology section (covering geo-archae-ology, paleo-botany and paleo-zoology) and that of Underwater Archaeology. Other innovations were the creation of new exhibition spaces, the reorganisation of the library (one of the most important archaeology libraries in the country), and the encouragement of acquisition and exchange schemes between archaeology libraries both in Portugal and abroad. Finally the museum journal, «O Arqueólogo Português», founded in 1895, was relaunched.

Apart from the obviously substantial archaeology and ethnology sections in the museum, other sections worthy of mention include those devoted to: precious metalwork, sculpture, mosaics, epigraphy, coins and medals, the Egyptian Collection, ethnography and African art.

Mosaic in the National Museum of Archaeology and Ethnology.

Praça de Afonso de Alburquerque and Palace of Belém.

CARRIAGE MUSEUM

Situated in Praça de Afonso de Alburquerque –Belém– this museum boasts the most varied collection of old carriages that the most demanding enthusiast could ever dream of. The vehicles, including particularly luxury coaches used in the 17th, 18th and 19th centuries, are a delight to behold, their sheer elegance magically erasing any feeling of anachronism. The principal carriages of the old Portuguese court are here in the museum, including the original vehicle used by Philip I of Portugal, the oldest in the collection, and the carriage of João V, the most impressive and luxurious.

The changing of the guard.

One of the carriages in the museum.

A view of the Carriage Museum.

Spanish tapestry room in the National Palace of Ajuda.

Don Joan IV room (National Palace of Ajuda). The paintings represent the acclamation of King Joan IV. ▷

NATIONAL PALACE OF AJUDA

Former royal residence, now used by the President of the Republic for official acts, construction of the National Palace of Ajuda began in 1802 and was completed some 31 years later according to the original plans drawn up by architects Francisco Xavier Fabri and José Da Costa.

The building occupies the site of an earlier palace made of wood and destroyed by fire in 1794. Ironically, this had been built to temporarily house the Portuguese royal family after the official residence of the monarchy, the Ribeira Palace, was destroyed in the 1755 earthquake.

The National Palace of Ajuda combines the baroque and neo-classical styles.

The entrance to the site is found in the centre of its limestone main front, in reality a side front according to the original plans. The three great windows on the upper floor are separated by Doric columns.

Inside, many of the sumptuous rooms still conserve the royal furniture as well as rich collections of objects brought here from other palaces. One of the outstanding features of the palace is the collection of some 50 marble statues in the vestibule.

Particularly interesting are the paintings on the walls and ceilings of the palace, the work of such artists as Vieira Portuense, Domingo Sequeira and Cirilo Machado. Also worthy of attention are the Persian carpets and Spanish tapestries which adorn the different rooms.

CITY MUSEUM

This museum is provisionally installed in the elegant Mitra Palace in Marvila, formerly the bishop's palace. In the entrance courtyard is a tomb dating from Roman times. The valuable contents of the City Museum allow visitors to recreate much of Lisbon's history and urban development. The collections of paintings, engravings, and documents relating to the city are particularly interesting, especially those dating from the 17th to the 19th century. The ethnographic collection is also noteworthy.

A view of the Alfama quarter, bas-relief in the City Museum.

BASILICA OF A ESTRELA

Also known as the Basilica of the Heart of Jesus, the construction of this building began in 1779 on the initiative of Dona Maria I, the wife of Royal Consort Pedro III after a vow she made if she bore a child. The architects in charge of the enterprise were Mateus Vicente and Manuel Reynaldos, who took their inspiration from the architectural lines of the convent at Mafra.

The façade of the Estrela Basilica consists of two

Basilica of A Estrela.

towers and a high dome and features allegorical figures and statues of saints sculpted by Machado de Castro.

The interior of the church is richly decorated, and on the high altar is a painting representing the heart of Jesus.

Here, in a glass coffin, is the body of Saint Exupério. Formerly in the catacombs of Rome, Pope Pius VI gave the holy remains to Portugal in 1791. Also of interest is the tomb of Queen Maria with its Latin inscriptions.

The Basilica da Estrela is a fine vantage point from which to contemplate splendid panoramic views of Lisbon stretching out towards the Tagus.

La Estrela Garden.

PALACE OF THE ASSEMBLY OF THE REPUBLIC

This building was formerly occupied by the Convent of São Bento. It was completely restored towards the end of the 18th century under the direction of the architect Ventura Terra in order to install the legislative chamber there. It again underwent alteration in 1935. The Palace of the Assembly of the Republic (Parliament) has a sumptuous front with a beautifully proportioned staircase leading up to it. Outstanding features inside the building include the Sala dos Passos Perdidos (waiting room), decorated by João Vaz e Columbano, who painted several portraits depicting well-known figures in Portuguese politicians, and the Assembly Hall, a wide semicircle of harmonious proportions decorated with paintings and sculptures. The Palace also houses the Torre do Tombo National Archive, a valuable collection containing such important works as *Don Duarte's Book of Hours*, dating to the 15th century, as well as a 16th-century Bible and 60 illustrated manuscripts of *Leitura Nova*.

Façade of the Palace of Assembly of the Republic.

The Santa Catarina mirador, *or viewpoint.*

THE VIEWPOINTS OF LISBON

Lisbon is a city of many vantage points. It could be said that the city, enchanted by her own beauty, takes pleasure in looking at herself in leisurely fashion from any one of the strategically placed belvederes which reflect her image.

The look-out point at St. George's Castle commands a vast panoramic view of great beauty, delightfully set out at different levels: São Vicente, the cathedral, the Mouraria district with its charming mediaeval structures, the Praça do Comerçio, Rossio, on one side, and on the other, Graça, the Monte de São Gens, the Penha de França, O Carmo, the Church of São Roque, Campolide, Almada, the fields of Ribatejo...

Another splendid vantage point is the one from São Pedro de Alcântara near to the Bairro Alto, overlooking the northern and eastern areas of Lisbon, with the smart Avenida da Liberdade at its feet.

There are further wonderful views to be seen from the viewpoints at Santa Luzia, close to St. George's Castle, and in the Alfama district, Monsanto, Senhora do Monte and Santa Catarina and in general, from any of the seventeen viewpoints overlooking the city.

Don José room and 18th-century silver objects in the Museum of Decorative Arts.

MUSEUM OF DECORATIVE ARTS

Belonging to the Ricardo Espirito Santo Foundation, this Museum is installed in a fine 17th-century palace at number 90, Calle de São Tomé. This palace, one of the oldest in Lisbon, formerly belonged to the counts of Arnoso. The contents of the Museum of Decorative Arts are made up of interesting collections of period furniture, valuable tapestries, ceramic objects, metal ornaments and historic engravings. The palace interior, which conserves its attractive original structure, and the tastefully decorated rooms, make this Museum a particularly evocative place to visit.

Another view of the Museum of Decorative Arts. ▷

Infante Don Henrique room, in the Military Museum.

MILITARY MUSEUM

Standing in the Largo do Museo de Artilharia, and founded in 1842, this is a most interesting museum which houses valuable collections of painting and sculpture, besides several pieces of artillery from different periods.

Also of note is the collection of military uniforms used by Portuguese soldiers in the African campaigns, the war against Napoleon and in the civil strife of the 19th century.

The different rooms in the Military Museum are specially designed to house the items making up the various collections, and all of these give us a histori-cal reflection of the development of military institutions in Portugal.

In a way, one might say that the patriotic spirit of the Portuguese nation is present here in the Military Museum, that admirable spirit that Camões wrote about in *Os Lusíadas,* as did Gil Vicente in the following verse:

Cobrai fame de ferozes,
Não de ricos, que é perigosa!
Dourai a pátria vossa
con mais nozes que vozes.
Avante, avante, Lisboa!

A view of the Vasco da Gama room.

Church of the Madre de Deus.

Interior of the Church of the Madre de Deus. ▷

THE CHURCH OF THE MOTHER OF GOD

This «Igreja da Madre de Deus» formerly belonged to the convent founded in 1509 by Queen Dona Leonor, widow of João II and the sister of King Don Manuel I, and was later restored by João III. It is one of the most splendid and evocative exponents of the religious architecture of the Manueline period, an outstanding age in the urban development of Lisbon. The Church of the Mother of God has a fine Manueline-style entrance emblazoned with the escutcheons of João II and Dona Leonor. The Renaissance-style cloister is worthy of special mention, with its interesting collection of historic glazed tiles in different colours, each more fascinating and original than the last.

The church was badly damaged as a result of the earthquake which devastated Lisbon in 1755 and was one of the buildings trapped between the city walls. The façade was not recovered until 1873, but was then restored on the lines of the model painted by Gregório Lopes in his famous triptych, now in the Museum of Ancient Art.

Inside the church, the large 18th-century nave is particularly outstanding. The chapel is splendid, too, and it also houses valuable paintings by early Portuguese artists and several relics, among them those of St. Ann, martyred in Cologne together with St. Gertrude and her 11,000 companions. Gregório Lopes painted the history of St. Ann and the arrival of her relics at Xabregas, and Maximilian of Austria offered these to Queen Leonor when she founded the convent of the Mother of God. The walls of the lower choir –the original chapel was built in the time

of Dona Leonor– are decorated with 16th-century tiles from Seville, and inside is an 18th-century reliquary. In the sacristy, which dates from the middle of the 17th century, are 16th-century paintings and several canvases by Gonçalves, dating to the 18th century.

The Church of the Mother of God is associated with the far-reaching transformation of the Portuguese capital brought about in the reign of Don Manuel I, and constitutes, though since altered, one of the most representative buildings of that splendid period in Portugal's history. Lisbon, at that time, was the capital of a great empire whose power was increasing and which covered practically the entire globe. Only two great monuments amongst Lisbon's outstanding Manueline edifices were left intact by the 1755 earthquake: Os Jerónimos and the Torre de Belém. Nevertheless, the Church of the Mother of God, which was partially saved, contributes with its presence to an evocation of the glory of the Lisbon devastated by that cataclysm.

Church of the Madre de Deus: choir.

Exterior of Lisbon's Campo Pequeno bullring.

BULLFIGHTING

This spectacle is deeply-rooted in Portugal, particularly in Ribatejo, but differs from the Spanish bullfight in that it is not permitted to kill the bull. Nevertheless, the struggle between man and bull offers a great deal of excitement and brilliance in the Portuguese arenas.

For bullfighting on horse-back, the gentlemen are dressed in 18th century costume, as it was during this period that the great bullfights became popularly accepted in Portugal.

The picturesque spectacle begins when the horsemen, «bandarilheiros» and «forcados» enter the arena. The members of the «quadrilha» stand in front of the presidential box and greet the authorities. Then the horsemen, tricorne in hand, trot around, saluting the public, their mounts performing to music various exercises of the Portuguese bullfighting school.

The Lisbon bullring, built in Spanish-Moorish style, is situated in Campo Pequeno, adjoining Avenida da Republica, and covers an area of 5,000 sq. metres.

Eduardo VII Park.

Marquis of Pombal Square. ▷

ESTUFA FRIA

Built in 1910, the Estufa Fria gardens are situated high up in the Eduardo VII Park. The designer of the project, Raul Carapinha –a famous Portuguese architect and painter– used the hollow in a rock found in the locality for the construction of the Estufa Fria. Extended in 1926, the gardens were officially inaugurated in 1930. Later on, a covered theatre building on soberly elegant lines was built at the highest point to serve as the venue for musical shows, dances, theatrical performances and the like.

In the Estufa Fria grow the loveliest and most varied botanical species from Portugal and tropical countries in a wonderful natural environment. This is a veritable paradise and a haven of peace and tranquillity, a genuinely idyllic oasis of plant life in the centre of the city.

This marvellous garden –a truly ideal spot– is protected from the outside by an original system of walls and beamed roofs which, sheltering it from the rigours of both winter and summer, keep the atmosphere at a steady temperature, preventing sudden changes. The name Estufa Fria («Cold Heater») alludes to these peculiar conditions.

The jungle-like nature of the garden is an infinite source of enchantment with its zigzagging paths, shady groves, bright pools, splashing waterfalls, rustic steps, poetic grottoes, miniature bridges and other elements, dotted by secluded nooks and corners like rooms covered by Nature with the sole purpose of providing shelter for Eros.

Islamic art gallery in the Gulbenkian Museum.

Silver-plated Egyptian mummy. ▷

GULBENKIAN MUSEUM

Created thanks to the generous bequest of Calouste Gulbenkian, the museum was opened to the public in 1969. Housed in an ultramodern building on the Avenida de Berna, it has an important collection of objects of the most diverse nature. The most interesting of these collections are the ivories and other examples of Moorish, mediaeval, Chinese and Japanese art, a collection of French painting and another of sculpture. Among the most noteworthy paintings in the Gulbenkian Museum are: *Portrait of an Old Man,* by Rembrandt, *Portrait of Helena Fourment,* by Rubens, and *The Man and the Doll,* by Degas.

Also fascinating are the collections of 18th and 19th century silver pieces, and the many magnificent examples of Regency, Louis XV and Louis XVI furniture.

The artistic heritage housed in this important Lisbon museum is based on the magnificent art collections amassed by Calouste Gulbenkian throughout forty fruitful years. The pieces forming part of the different collections, spanning from 2,800 years BC to the 20th century, are set out splendidly in the museum spaces.

To enable visitors to better appreciate the museum and its content, there are two circuits. The first of these is devoted to Oriental Art collections and features original works from Egypt, Syria, the Islamic Orient, and the Far East, as well as collections of Graeco-Roman works.

Gulbenkian Foundation: Auditorium.

13th-century Persian prayer niche. ▷

For its part, the second circuit features European art, including particularly collections of painting, sculpture, tapestries, jewellery, ivory, glass, coins, and furniture.

The Gulbenkian Museum also has a fine library, exhibition gallery and large lecture halls.

The Foundation created by Calouste Gulbenkian at number 45 Avenida de Berna, publishes two important magazines: *Colóquio/Artes* and *Colóquio/Letras.*

The first, published five times per year, is beautifully printed on embossed paper and illustrated with artistic reproductions in black and white and colour. Its pages contain essays by reputed international specialists on the subjects of painting, sculpture, music, the cinema and engraving, with a lengthy final section featuring reviews of the most important artistic events on the international scene.

The second of these two magazines, *Colóquio/Letras,* also splendidly-produced, features items contributed by important Portuguese intellectuals and writers, along with authors from other countries. It publishes essays, stories, poems and literary criticism.

This magazine devotes special attention to Portuguese and Brazilian letters, but is also open to literary trends from France, Spain, Italy, Poland and other countries.

Both the Museum and the publications of the Calouste Gulbenkian Foundation form splendid exponents of the art and culture of Portugal.

THE ZOOLOGICAL GARDENS

Situated in Palhavã, this Zoo is undoubtedly one of the most outstanding of its kind in the world. It stands not far from the Instituto de Oncologia in Quinta das Laranjeiras, a lovely estate that used to belong to the Count of Farrobo and is now owned by the State. The Avenida de Berna is near by, as is the Parque de Palhavã. Here stands the palace built by the Count of Sarzedas in the mid-17th century, where Queen Maria Francisca of Savoy died in 1683, and which is now the seat of the Calouste Gulbenkian Foundation.

The Zoo has a fine collection of the most varied types of animals from the most distant lands and from all the climates under the sun. Lisbon's Zoo is one of the most complete and fascinating in the whole of Europe. Lions, hippopotamuses, monkeys of different species, and many other animals live in this vast Zoological Garden.

Another interesting feature of the zoological gardens is the collection of floral species from many countries, including the marvellous specimens in the lovely rose garden, which are particularly outstanding.

Some seven kilometres from the Zoological Gardens is the Benfica residential area, where luxuriant vegetation also grows. In Praça de São Domingos Square stands the church of the convent of the same name, where lie the mortal remains of the Viceroy of India, Don João de Castro, and of Don João das Regras.

Lisbon Zoo.

Oporto wines.

GASTRONOMY

Lisbon is a city where you can eat extremely well and at reasonable prices. Cod is the Portuguese dish par *excellence.* It must be added that the cod is always top quality, specially cured to give it an unmistakable delicious taste. It is usually cooked with potatoes and garnished with oil or, in the most authentic of local dishes, roast with potatoes, onions, garlic and olives. White *vinho verde* wine forms an excellent accompaniment for either of these dishes.

Another important dish in Lisbon's gastronomic repertoire is *cozido à portuguesa,* Portuguese stew, made from chicken, beef, *enchido* sausage, pork, potatoes, cabbage, green beans and rice. An mature local red wine goes extremely well with this rich, succulent dish.

Iscas is another typical dish of the Lisbon area, made from liver –cut into fine slices and macerated in white wine and vinegar– fried with bacon and garnished with boiled potatoes.

The exquisite sardines, grilled and accompanied by boiled potatoes, are popular in Lisbon, where we can also find such other fish of the highest quality as red mullet, sole, hake, and the most varied and tasty shellfish, including crab and lobster, barnacles, cockles, scampi and prawns.

The local cheeses –fresh or matured– and the magnificent fruit of Portugal form an unmatched dessert.

As for wines, red and white, young and mature alike, these are excellent throughout the country and not too strong, fine-tasting with a slight after-taste.

Folklore. Fado *singers.*

LISBON'S FOLKLORE

Among the rich and evocative folklore of Lisbon, the fado occupies the place of honour. The *fado* is an essentially sentimental song, the lyrical expression of the Portuguese soul, mingled with feelings of fatality, sadness and hope, deriving, according to some authors, from mediaeval Portuguese song and Mozarabic *jaryas.* In the delightful cadence of the fado one finds a harmonious combination of nostalgia for the past and lament for present adversity. The *fado* became popular in the 18th century when the *cantadeiras,* with their black dresses and black shawls, and the *cantadores,* accompanied by the melancholy notes of violas and guitars, began to perform them in the typical cafes of the Bairro Alto and Alfama districts.

Another singular element of Lisbon's folklore is the celebration of the Ladra Fair, where everything from the seemingly most useless of objects to valuable works of art are sold, including new and second-hand clothes, shoes, pottery, books... It is a colourful scene, described in verse by Henrique O'Neill during the last century:

Salve, três veces, venerável feira!
Derradeiro degrau que o artefacto,
Cumprindo a lei inexorável, cega,
Que impérios, tribos, monumentos, choças,
Astros, boninas condenou à morte,
Desce para voltar a ser mesquinha
Matéria-prima de futuras obras!

The feast days of the «Popular Saints» (St. John, St. Anthony, and St. Peter), which take place in the month of June in the Alfama district, also offer an extraordinarily dynamic spectacle which leaves visitors with an indelible memory.

Nor must we forget the «Feira Popular», of course, a site with many bars and restaurants of all kinds, including the «Café dos Pretos» particularly outstanding for its exquisite coffee and the originality of its African decor, where grilled sardines and chicken are eaten in the open air, amid a gay, festive spirit, an air of overflowing vitality filling summer nights in Lisbon with fun and excitement.

Lisbon folklore.

Front of the Queluz Palace.

THE NATIONAL PALACE OF QUELUZ

A former royal residence, this magnificent palace is only a few kilometres from Lisbon, in the town of Queluz. It is a sumptuous building dating from the second half of the 18th century, designed by the Portuguese architect Mateus Vicente and the Frenchman Robillon. It has been justifiably referred to as the Portuguese Versailles. Indeed, the «ceremonial» façade opens onto beautiful gardens in the style of Versailles. The façade of the royal chamber and the noble sweep of the Lions' staircase are also of interest.

Inside the National Palace of Queluz, the following elements are particularly noteworthy: the so-called Casa de Mangas, whose walls are decorated with glazed tiles by Rato depicting the discoveries made by the Portuguese in different parts of the world; the Reception Gallery –the Ambassadors' Chamber– whose ceiling features a painting depicting a concert in the court of Don João V, its walls faced with marble and mirrors; the Council of State Chamber, on its ceiling a painting symbolising Time, attributed to Pedro Alexandrino; the King's Chamber –also known as the Don Quixote Chamber– decorated with scenes from «Don Quixote», painted by Manuel da Costa and J. A. Narciso, with a pictorial allegory of the Arts on the ceiling. In this room is conserved the bed belonging to Pedro IV; the Sala das Merendas with 18th century paintings; the Oratory of the Princesses Maria Jose and Maria Dorotela; the Sala de Lanternem, with the portrait of King Don Miguel, by Ender; the Music Room, with three lovely Venetian crystal candelabra and

Queleuz Palace: Throne Room.

ceiling painted in green and pink; and the Throne Room, in Louis XV style, decorated by Jose Vicente and Silvestre de Faria.

The Queleuz gardens are most interesting, particularly the Garden of Neptune, designed by Robillon in the style of Le Nôtre, and which stretches out through a terrace of archways separated from the park by a balustrade with statues by Manuel Alves and Silvestre de Faria, and the Dos Azereiros garden, dating from the time Marshall Junot installed himself in the palace after Napoleon's troops had invaded Portuguese territory.

Ambassadors' Chamber in the Queleuz Palace.

ESTORIL

Estoril is where the so-called Portuguese Riviera really begins. This is a first class tourist centre with modern hotels, swimming pools, golf courses, tennis courts, riding schools, a sailing club and amenities for every type of sport.

The many tourist attractions to be found in Estoril during the day include particularly its wonderful beaches, whilst at night the outstanding attraction is the famous Casino, standing on the highest point in the Park. Here, in addition to other amusements, are gaming rooms where one can try one's luck at roulette or baccarat. Estoril has a mild climate and boasts truly delightful countryside.

Two partial views of Estoril beach.

Partial view of the beach at Cascais.

CASCAIS

A former fishing village some three kilometres from Estoril, Cascais is now one of Portugal's most flourishing tourist resorts. The citadel of Cascais was the summer residence of the Portuguese monarchs from 1871 to 1910. Along its walls stretches the Passeio de Santo Antonio, with two superimposed terraces fringed by elegant palm trees.

Situated on the so-called Portuguese Costa do Sol in an impressive bay, Cascais boasts many excellent hotels and restaurants. Various houses, surrounded by lovely gardens, dating from the time when the court spent the summers in Cascais, are still conserved here.

La Guía Lighthouse, in Cascais.

National Palace, Sintra.

SINTRA

Overlooking the majestic mountain range that bears its name and whose magnificent vegetation Byron described as «glorious Eden» in his poem Childe Harold, Sintra, with its fantastic park, its two royal palaces and its ancient castle, the Castelo dos Mouros, is one of the loveliest romantic scenes imaginable. Its delightful personality and the incomparable scenery around it are of an indescribable charm and beauty. Sintra is unique, incomparable. It is impossible even to reflect a pale image of its unequalled loveliness. Sintra has be seen, its beauty and many enchantments absorbed by the spirit.

The outstanding monuments of Sintra include particularly the Royal Palace, which stands in the main square and is a building of the highest artistic value. Architecturally embracing various styles, it was the residence of the Portuguese monarchs from the 15th century. Its illustrious historical past witnessed the voice of Camões reciting the verses of *Os Lusíadas* before the king, as well as the laments of Afonso VI, the unfortunate monarch whose own brother shut him up in a wing of the palace after taking away his wife and his throne.

The marvellous Parque da Pena, with its steep shaded walks, splashing fountains and century-old trees is one of Sintra's greatest attractions. «*Today* –exclaimed Richard Strauss enthusiastically when he came to Sintra– *is the happiest day of my life! I know Italy, Sicily, Greece, and Egypt, but I have never seen anything like Pena. It's the loveliest thing I've ever seen!*»

In the heights of Sintra is the Pena Palace –a privileged vantage-point commanding magnificent mountain views– with its curious Dragon gateway, its bell towers and minarets, its domes and sentry walks, Manueline style windows with capricious ogee arches and a fascinating mixture of styles.

There is also a fine view from the mediaeval Castelo dos Mouros, with the blue sea on one side and the convent at Mafra, one of the most majestic monuments in Portugal, on the other.

Palace of A Pena.

Overall view of Sesimbra.

SESIMBRA

An important fishing port and spa, Sesimbra offers the charm of its welcoming nearby beaches and the attraction of the delicious fish to be eaten in its restaurants.

The public auction of the fish caught by the fishermen of Sesimbra is a highly picturesque sight. The whole town has maintained completely intact its delightful image of a small fishing town.

The parish church is of interest, featuring 17th-century paintings depicting scenes from the popular festivity of Our Lady of the Wounds, which has been held on the May 3 and 4 here since the 16th century.

SETUBAL

This town, formerly called *Cetobriga,* is situated on the left bank of the mouth of the River Sado and has now become an important industrial city. Also one of the most important fishing ports in the country, it has the largest canning industry in Portugal. There are also prosperous cement and phosphate factories here. Setúbal's main street is the Avenida de Luisa Todi, named after the famous Portuguese singer, which runs parallel to the river. Nearby are a park and a Theatre which go by the same name, and the Oceanographic Museum with some interesting collections including a particularly fine one of sea sponges.

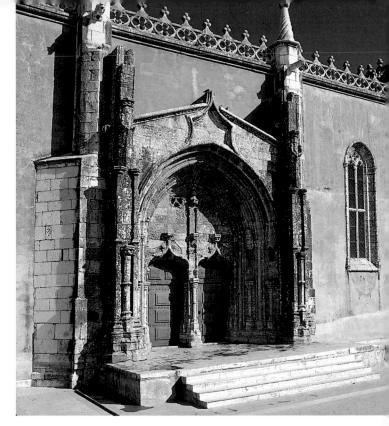

Portal of the Church of Jesus of Setúbal.

Of the monuments to be found in Setúbal, the most noteworthy, is the Church of Jesus, built in the late-15th century by the same architect who directed work on the Monastery of the Jerónimos. It is a fine example of Gothic architecture with Manueline style additions. The portico is made from Arrabida marble. Inside, the walls are faced with beautiful 17th-century tiles, some featuring scenes from the life of the Virgin. The Manueline style cloister is also of interest. Other churches worthy of mention are those of São Julião, rebuilt at the beginning of the 16th century, and Santa Maria da Graça, dating from the 13th century, rebuilt in the 16th century and beautifully decorated with 18th century tiles.

View of Setúbal from Saint Philip's Castle.

CONTENTS

EDITORIAL ESCUDO DE ORO, S.A.
I.S.B.N. 84-378-0468-X
Printed by FISA - Escudo de Oro, S.A.
Legal Dep. B. 2094-2000

ESCUDO DE ORO, S.A. COLLECTIONS

ALL SPAIN

1 MADRID
2 BARCELONA
3 SEVILLE
4 MAJORCA
5 THE COSTA BRAVA
8 CORDOBA
9 GRANADA
10 VALENCIA
11 TOLEDO
12 SANTIAGO
13 IBIZA and Formentera
14 CADIZ and provincia
15 MONTSERRAT
16 CANTABRIA
17 TENERIFE
20 BURGOS
21 ALICANTE
24 SEGOVIA
25 SARAGOSSA
26 SALAMANCA
27 AVILA
28 MINORCA
29 SAN SEBASTIAN and Guipúzcoa
30 ASTURIAS
31 LA CORUNNA and the Rías Altas
32 TARRAGONA
40 CUENCA
41 LEON
42 PONTEVEDRA, VIGO and Rías Bajas
43 RONDA
46 SIGUENZA
47 ANDALUSIA
52 EXTREMADURA
54 MORELLA
58 VALLDEMOSSA

GUIDES

1 MADRID
2 BARCELONA
3 LA RIOJA
4 MAJORCA
6 SANTIAGO DE COMPOSTELA
7 SEVILLA
8 ANDALUCIA
9 GRAN CANARIA
12 GALICIA
13 CORDOBA
14 COSTA BLANCA
15 GRANADA
22 SEGOVIA
25 AVILA
26 HUESCA
28 TOLEDO
30 SANTANDER

---

4 LONDON

---

1 LA HABANA VIEJA
2 EL CAPITOLIO (CUBA)
3 NECROPOLIS DE LA HABANA (CUBA)

ALL EUROPE

1 ANDORRA
2 LISBON
3 LONDON
4 BRUGES
6 MONACO
7 VIENNA
11 VERDUN
12 THE TOWER OF LONDON
13 ANTWERP
14 WESTMINSTER ABBEY
15 THE SPANISH RIDING
   SCHOOL IN VIENNA
17 WINDSOR CASTLE
18 LA CÔTE D'OPAL
19 COTE D'AZUR
22 BRUSSELS
23 SCHÖNBRUNN PALACE
26 HOFBURG PALACE
27 ALSACE
28 RHODES
32 PERPIGNAN
33 STRASBOURG
34 MADEIRA + PORTO SANTO
35 CERDAGNE - CAPCIR
36 BERLIN
37 MOSCU
38 PORTUGAL

TOURISM

1 COSTA DEL SOL
2 COSTA BRAVA
3 ANDORRA
4 ANTEQUERA
6 MENORCA
8 MALLORCA
9 TENERIFE
14 LA ALPUJARRA
15 LA AXARQUIA
16 PARQUE ARDALES AND EL CHORRO
17 NERJA
18 GAUDI
19 BARCELONA
21 MARBELLA
23 LA MANGA DEL MAR MENOR
25 CATEDRAL DE LEON
26 MONTSERRAT
28 PICASSO
34 RONDA
35 IBIZA-FORMENTERA
37 GIRONA
38 CADIZ
39 ALMERIA
40 SAGRADA FAMILIA
41 FUENGIROLA
42 FATIMA
43 LANZAROTE
44 MEZQUITA HASSAN II
45 JEREZ DE LA FRONTERA
46 PALS
47 VALLDEMOSSA
48 SANTILLANA DEL MAR
49 LA ALHAMBRA Y EL GENERALIFE
51 MONACO-MONTECARLO

ALL AMERICA

1 PUERTO RICO
2 SANTO DOMINGO
3 QUEBEC
4 COSTA RICA
5 CARACAS
6 LA HABANA

---

1 CUZCO
2 AREQUIPA
3 LIMA
4 MACHU PICCHU

ALL AFRICA

1 MOROCCO
3 TUNISIA

ART IN SPAIN

1 PALAU DE LA MUSICA CATALANA
2 GAUDI
3 PRADO MUSEUM I
   (Spanish Painting)
4 PRADO MUSEUM I
   (Foreing Painting)
5 MONASTERY OF GUADALUPE
7 THE FINE ARTS MUSUEM OF SEVILLE
10 THE CATHEDRAL OF GIRONA
11 GRAN TEATRO DEL LICEO
   (Great Opera House
22 MEZQUITA DE CORDOBA
14 PICASSO
15 ROYAL PALACE OF SEVILLE
19 THE ALHAMBRA AND THE GENERALIFE
21 ROYAL ESTATE OF ARANJUEZ
22 ROYAL ESTATE OF EL PARDO
24 ROYAL PALACE OF SAN ILDEFONSO
26 OUR LADY OF THE PILLAR OF
   SARAGOSSA
27 TEMPLE DE LA SAGRADA FAMILIA
28 POBLET ABTEI
29 THE CATHEDRAL OF SEVILLE
30 THE CATHEDRAL DE MAJORCA
32 CARTUJA DE VALLDEMOSSA
33 GOYA
34 THE CATHEDRAL OF BARCELONA
35 CASA - MUSEU CASTELL GALA-DALI
   PUBOL
36 THE CATHEDRAL OF SIGUENZA
37 SANTA MARIA LA REAL DE NAJERA
38 CASA - MUSEU SALVADOR DALI
   PORT LLIGAT

MONOGRAPHS (S)

5 SOLAR ENERGY IN THE CERDAGNE
10 MORELLA
20 CAPILLA REAL DE GRANADA
31 CORDILLERAS DE PUERTO RICO
38 GIBRALTAR
50 BRUGES
68 MONASTERIO DE PIEDRA
70 TORREVIEJA
74 VALLDEMOSSA
75 ANTWERP
84 CATHEDRAL OF MAJORCA
85 CATHEDRAL OF BARCELONA
86 VALL D'UXO

MONOGRAPHS (L)

5 PUERTO RICO
6 THE OLD SAN JUAN
9 THE CITY OF BRUGES
19 MURALLAS DE SAN JUAN

MAPS

1 MADRID
2 BARCELONA
6 LONDON
8 ALICANTE
20 PANAMA
31 SEVILLE
33 BRUGES
34 BRUSSELS
35 ANTWERP
36 SEGOVIA
37 CORDOBA
38 CADIZ
40 PALMA OF MAJORCA
45 JEREZ DE LA FRONTERA
47 AVILA
48 ANDORRA
50 SALAMANCA
52 LEON
53 BURGOS
58 IBIZA
59 OOSTENDE
78 GRANADA
80 MONACO
93 MENORCA
94 LA MANGA DEL MAR MENOR
96 COSTA BRAVA
97 MADEIRA
98 SANTANDER
99 LLORET DE MAR
100 ANDALUCIA
101 JAEN

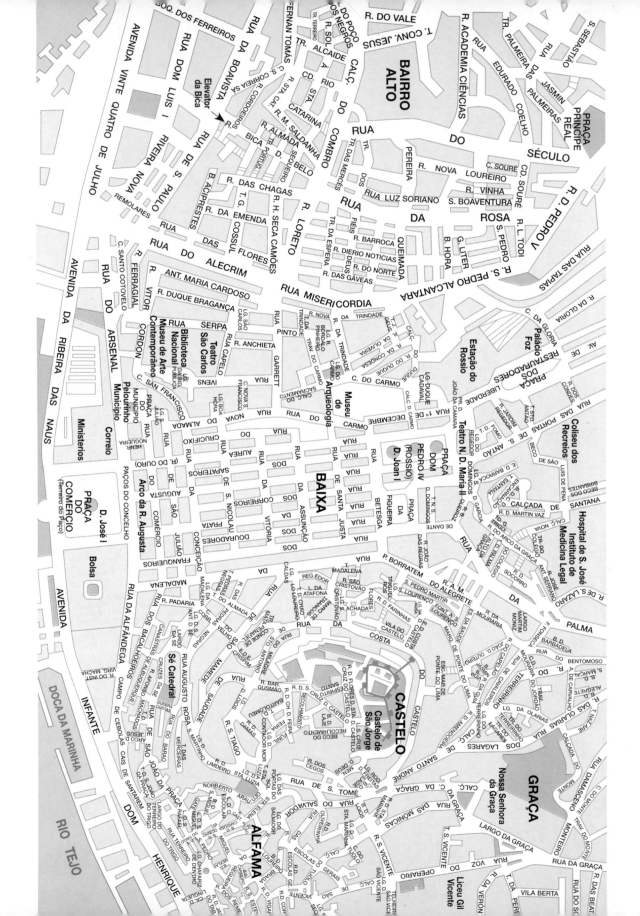